Entrusting Your Dreams to God

BY JUDITH COUCHMAN

Bible Studies

Daring to Be Different: A Study on Deborah
Becoming a Woman God Can Use: A Study on Esther
Entrusting Your Dreams to God: A Study on Hannah
Choosing the Joy of Obedience: A Study on Mary
Celebrating Friendship
His Gentle Voice (Bible study in the book)
Designing a Woman's Life Bible Study
Why Is Her Life Better Than Mine?
If I'm So Good, Why Don't I Act That Way?
Getting a Grip on Guilt

Books

The Shadow of His Hand
His Gentle Voice
A Garden's Promise
The Woman Behind the Mirror
Shaping a Woman's Soul
Designing a Woman's Life
Lord, Please Help Me to Change
Lord, Have You Forgotten Me?

Compilations

Encouragement for the Heart
Psalm 23
Amazing Grace
Voices of Faith
Promises for Spirit-Led Living
Cherished Thoughts about Friendship
Cherished Thoughts about Love
Cherished Thoughts about Prayer
Breakfast for the Soul
One Holy Passion

Life Messages of Great Christians Series

His Redeeming Love (Jonathan Edwards)
The Way of Faith (Martin Luther)
Called to Commitment (Watchman Nee)
Growing in Grace (John Wesley)
The Promise of Power (Jamie Buckingham)
Only Trust Him (Dwight L. Moody)
For Me to Live Is Christ (Charles Spurgeon)
Growing Deeper with God (Oswald Chambers)
Dare to Believe (Smith Wigglesworth)
Anywhere He Leads Me (Corrie ten Boom)
Loving God with All Your Heart (Andrew Murray)
A Very Present Help (Amy Carmichael)

WOMEN OF FAITH™
BIBLE STUDY SERIES

Women of the Bible

Entrusting Your
Dreams to God

A Study on Hannah

Judith Couchman

Foreword by Sheila Walsh

ZONDERVAN™

GRAND RAPIDS, MICHIGAN 49530 USA

For Cindy Miller,
who believed in dreams with me

ZONDERVAN™

Entrusting Your Dreams to God
Formerly titled *Hannah*
Copyright © 1999 by Women of Faith, Inc.

Judith Couchman, General Editor

Requests for information should be addressed to:

Zondervan, *Grand Rapids, Michigan 49530*

ISBN 0-310-24783-7

Portions of the fiction pieces have been adapted from *His Gentle Voice* © 1998 by Judith Couchman. Used by permission of Multnomah Publishers, Inc.

All Scripture quotations, unless otherwise indicated, are taken from the *Holy Bible: New International Version*®. NIV®. Copyright © 1973, 1978, 1984 by International Bible Society. Used by permission of Zondervan. All rights reserved.

Interior design by Sherri Hoffman

Printed in the United States of America

03 04 05 06 / ❖ CH/ 10 9 8 7 6 5 4 3

Contents

Acknowledgments   7

Foreword   8

About This Study   10

Introduction   13

SESSION ONE: The Object of Great Desire   15
   God plants "impossible" dreams deep in the soul.

SESSION TWO: A Matter of the Heart   26
   Before God changes circumstances, he changes us.

SESSION THREE: A Promise Kept   37
   A vow to the Creator is a pledge to remember.

SESSION FOUR: The Source of Strength   46
   The Lord deserves honor for dreams come true.

SESSION FIVE: A Lifetime of Letting Go   55
   Living the dream means learning to surrender.

SESSION SIX: A Lingering Influence   64
   God uses our dreams to serve his purposes.

Leader's Guide   73

Acknowledgments

Many thanks to Ann Spangler, senior editor for Zondervan, for giving me the opportunity to write about Hannah, and to Christine Anderson and Lori Walburg for their expert editing. Also to Charette Barta, Opal Couchman, Win Couchman, Madalene Harris, Karen Hilt, Shirley Honeywell, and Nancy Lemons — all women who are available to God, especially through prayer.

Foreword

This is an amazing story! Hannah was a dynamic "woman of faith." The culture that she grew up in is foreign to us, but her life and her devotion to God reach through the pages of his Word and challenge us to live a life of beauty and honor.

I talk to many women who carry the pain of being unable to have a child. "If God loves me so much, why does he ignore my prayers?" they ask. I can hold these women in my arms and weep with them, but I know and they know that I have a darling little boy at home. Hannah, however, would look at these women, and they would see in her eyes a depth of empathy and pain because she has walked that lonely valley too.

I received a letter from a woman who told me that she finds Christmas unbearable. It's the tradition in her family for all the children and grandchildren to gather in her parents' home on Christmas Eve. She wrote, "I watch my sister's children running through the house, chasing the cat, laughing, and my husband and I stand there with empty arms." Hannah would understand. She was one of two wives, and Peninnah, the other wife, had children, a reality that she loved to throw in Hannah's face.

But Hannah's story is much more than the story of a woman who wanted to have a child. Whatever you are facing in your life right now, Hannah has something to say to you. She was in a desperate situation. She was carrying an unbearable burden. In her despair she called out to God. In fact, she was praying so earnestly and with such emotion that the priest thought she was drunk! I'm amazed that she didn't just give up and go home. Have you ever felt like that? That no matter what you try to do with the best heart in the world, no one understands you at all? But Hannah didn't give up, and God answered her prayer.

I can imagine the joy in her eyes when she first held that little boy in her arms. But Hannah had made a promise to God. She told him that if he gave her a child she would give him back to God to serve him in the very temple where she had prayed. Would she be able to keep her promise having kissed that little cheek and watched him as he slept?

This is a life-changing story. Throw yourself into this study with heart and soul, and you will be a different woman at the end.

— *Sheila Walsh*

About This Study

*E*veryone loves a captivating story. It can prompt laughter, tears, nods of the head, even thoughtful silence. Best of all, a good story teaches us how to live better. It doles out guidelines, points to pitfalls, and inspires us toward heart-changing action. It infuses the ordinary with meaning and the tragic with truth.

In this Women of Faith discussion guide you'll explore one of those poignant stories. Through the life of Hannah, a biblical woman with an intriguing dilemma, you'll learn how God can work in the world, in the lives of his people, and in your circumstances. Each of the six sessions unfolds her story, compares it to yours, and initiates a group discussion that will invoke spiritual growth and life-related applications.

To most effectively utilize this discussion guide with your group, consider organizing your time as follows.

BEFORE A GROUP SESSION

Before attending a meeting, take time alone to evaluate your life and prepare for the next group discussion. During this time read and ponder the following sections of the discussion guide.

- *Opening Narrative.* Each week you'll be ushered into another chapter of Hannah's story. This fiction narrative introduces her unusual circumstances and helps you envision how Hannah felt, and perhaps what she did, as the events around her unfolded. It can get you thinking about the story before the group assembles, and whet your appetite for what happens next.

- *Setting the Stage.* Based on Hannah's story and the session's theme, think about your life. The questions and suggested activities can help you consider the following: How am I doing in this area? How do I feel about it? What do I want to do or change? How does this affect my spiritual life? Be honest with yourself and God, asking him to teach you through Hannah's story.

DURING YOUR TIME TOGETHER

The heart of this guide focuses on gathering for discussion and encouragement. It allows time to study the Bible, apply its truths to your lives, and pray together. Of course, you can add whatever else fits the nature of your group, such as time for a "coffee klatch" and catching up on each other's lives. Whatever you decide, reserve about an hour for these four sections.

- *Discussing Hannah's Story.* In this section you will read and discuss a biblical passage that captures the remarkable events of Hannah's life. Though the discussion centers on the facts of God's Word, at times you'll read between the lines and suggest people's feelings, motivations, and character qualities to gain insights to their actions. Still, you can answer these questions without compromising the biblical text.

    To best manage this discussion time, you can follow these steps:

    1. Ask one woman to read out loud the opening narrative, if it seems appropriate. If not, skip this step.
    2. As a group, read aloud the Bible text stated at the beginning of the section. Take turns reading verses so each woman participates.
    3. Discuss the questions together, consulting specific verses from the text as needed.

- *Behind the Scenes.* This section provides background information related to the biblical text. It enlightens the story's culture and history, and helps you answer the discussion questions. You can refer to this section as you discuss Hannah's story.
- *Sharing Your Story.* How does Hannah's story apply to your life? As a group you can answer that question, relating the events of her life to your own and uncovering nuggets of practical application. These questions target group sharing rather than personal contemplation.
- *Prayer Matters.* To conclude your session use these ideas to guide the group in prayer, especially focusing on individual needs.

AFTER A MEETING

Since spiritual growth doesn't end with your small group gathering, try these suggestions to extend learning into the next week and encourage one-on-one relationships. However, these sections are optional, depending on your interest and schedule.

- *After Hours.* These activities help apply the lesson's principles to everyday life. You can complete them with a friend or by yourself.
- *Words to Remember.* After you return home, memorize the selected Bible verses for encouragement and guidance.

In addition, the back of the book presents a Leader's Guide to help your group's facilitator pilot the discussion. To ensure that everyone contributes to the conversation, it's best to keep the group at six to eight participants. If the membership increases, consider splitting into smaller groups during the discussion times and gathering together for the concluding prayer.

However you organize the meeting, keep the emphasis on discussion — sharing ideas, needs, and questions, rather than striving for a consensus of opinion. That's the pleasure of a good story. It stimulates thinking and reflects our inner selves so along with Hannah we can become women of faith.

— Judith Couchman, General Editor

Introduction

$\mathscr{H}$ave you ever wanted something so much you lay awake at night just thinking about it? Have you ever tearfully blurted an unfulfilled dream to friends? Or felt you'd burst from the pain of a constant, throbbing desire?

Then you'll love Hannah's story. The Bible says Hannah wept about her barrenness and begged the Lord to give her a child. She cried loud and long about her emptiness and used words like *misery* and *anguish* to describe her feelings. She didn't hold back with God, pretending it didn't hurt. She felt "bitterness of soul" and told him about it. (See 1 Samuel 1:10–11, 16.)

Did God disapprove of Hannah's honest approach?

Not at all. The Lord not only gave her a son, he blessed her with six children.

This is good news for those of us who feel we have to say the right words or be a stiff-upper-lip Christian to receive good gifts from God. It's a relief to know we can pour out our hearts to the Creator who hears and answers prayer.

On the other hand, like Hannah we may have to wait for God's answer longer than we expect or want to. His timing differs from ours, for reasons we may never know or understand. So can we entrust our dreams to God as we wait? Or even more, will we?

This discussion guide can help your group answer these questions and others, exploring how to both humbly and actively wait for God to fulfill a dream. Or if you don't have a dream but long to cull one from deep within, you can discuss trusting the Lord to give you a vision for your life. Together, you'll explore:

- Living with "impossible" dreams tucked in our hearts.
- Changing ourselves before changing our circumstances.
- Keeping committed and fulfilling our promises.
- Giving God credit for dreams come true.
- Learning to obey as we "live the dream."
- Using our dreams to serve God's purposes.

Still, we don't have to be in agony to learn from Hannah's life. In many ways, hers is every woman's story, an encouraging picture of how God wants to bless those who truly follow him. Even those who may not, right now, have a specific dream tucked in their hearts.

A contemporary theologian has remarked that humility is absolute dependence on and trust in God, with the consequent ability to move mountains. So whether you're struggling with an unfulfilled dream, clueless about a vision for yourself, excited about a good idea, or happily working toward your heart's desire, you can learn to entrust your life to God.

— Judith Couchman

The Object of Great Desire

*God plants "impossible" dreams
deep in the soul.*

*H*annah was a desperate woman.

Year after year, when she packed for the annual trip to Shiloh with her husband, Elkanah, her heart filled with dread. There they would present sacrifices and offerings to the Lord in his house. There they would celebrate Jehovah's goodness to them. There, once again, Hannah would feel humiliated.

"But why?" asked Elkanah, cupping Hannah's face in his weathered hands and kissing the lips he adored. "Why are you so sad? Why can't you enjoy our trip to the holy temple?"

Hannah tried to explain, for she deeply loved her husband, but the words jumbled and her eyes puddled with tears. Moving his hands to Hannah's back and pulling her to his chest, Elkanah implored, "Why, my dear wife?"

With her head tucked under his chin, she sobbed, "I speak to the Lord, but he doesn't talk to me. Nor does he answer my pleas for a child."

Elkanah sighed and kissed the top of Hannah's head. "Don't I mean more to you than ten sons?" he asked quietly.

"You are everything a husband can mean to a wife," she answered. "But I can't extinguish my desire to conceive. It burns within me."

Hannah was not ungrateful to Elkanah for his attention, or for his husbandly protection and provision. Many women in her hill community endured their marriages; their spouses treated them as mere chattel, as objects to own rather than lovers to cherish. But not Elkanah. He delighted in Hannah and favored her.

Each year when he sacrificed to the Lord, Elkanah gave portions of the meat to his other wife, Peninnah, and to all her sons and daughters. But to Hannah he gave a double portion as a symbol of his enduring love, even with Peninnah's jealous eyes watching him. Even though Hannah bore him no children.

Yet as much as he tried, Elkanah couldn't understand the depth of Hannah's pain. The maternal instinct, deep as the soul itself. The shame when neighbors insinuated her barrenness was God's curse for some secret sin. The taunting from that "other woman" in Elkanah's life who plentifully bore him heirs and sneered at Hannah's infertility. The desire to complete her marriage — to express her love with the greatest gift she could give, the birth of a son.

Whatever the reason for his perplexity, Hannah needed more than Elkanah's soothing words. For the pain within, for the barrenness of her womb, she needed to hear from God.

Setting the Stage

WHAT DO YOU WANT?

Do you harbor an unfulfilled desire that won't diminish? Before meeting with the group, take time to privately pour out your feelings on paper. Whether in the space provided, in a journal or on a computer, honestly describe your longing. For example:

- What do you want? Why?

- How do you feel about not having it?

- How do you feel about yourself?

- How do you feel about God?

- What hopeful feelings do you have?

- Why has this dream stayed alive?

Write out the questions that you hide inside. If you feel wistful or silly, sad or angry, hurt or hopeful, puzzled or disbelieving, say so.

Now be a dreamer. Write out a description or draw a picture of your life if you obtained this object of desire. Don't edit your dream or feelings. How would you feel? What would you do? How would it affect others? How would you feel about God?

But what if you don't have a dream? You're not alone. Many of us would like to have a dream for our lives, but don't. As you attend the discussion sessions, you can use them as motivation to ask God to give you a vision for your life. In the meantime, you can relax and simply soak in the information for future use.

At the same time, living without a dream can feel just as perplexing and purposeless as living with an unfulfilled dream. If you don't have a dream but wish you did, write out how you feel about it. Is it painful? Or do you not care? Have you given up hope? Or is there a desire for a dream, but you don't know where to begin? Tell God. Write a prayer about how you feel, and if you're ready, ask him to place his dreams in your heart.

Whether you have a dream or need one, gather up your courage and wish big. Hannah did.

Discussing Hannah's Story

DESIRE TURNED INTO DILEMMA

Hannah's desire for a baby coursed so powerfully through her, it couldn't be contained. The longing spilled out through her tears, through her words and actions, onto those she loved and loathed. Like a wild river, it flooded every crevice of her life, threatening to drown her hope and happiness.

Still, childbirth wasn't an unusual dream for a young Jewish wife. In her culture motherhood was normal, expected. Unfortunately, this "normal expectation" opened the floodgate of Hannah's unfulfilled desire and created a crisis.

Before you begin the discussion, read the Bible text, 1 Samuel 1:1–8.

1. To better understand Hannah's dilemma, turn to the Behind the Scenes section called "The Blessing of Barrenness" on page 20 and ask one woman to read it aloud. Given this insight to her culture's

view of barrenness, how might Hannah have felt about herself and her dream? List your answers on a whiteboard or easel pad so everyone can see and discuss them.

2. First Samuel 1:5–6 claims that the Lord closed Hannah's womb. It's unclear whether Hannah knew this or whether the author added this comment in hindsight. If Hannah knew that God designed her barrenness, how would it add to the feelings your group listed in question one? Why would God choose to close Hannah's womb? Explore more than one reason.

3. Hannah not only struggled with her own feelings, but also endured the taunting "other wife" who lived with her. Read verses 6 and 7. What do they reveal about the characters of Hannah and Peninnah? Do you think each woman's attitudes and actions were justified? Why or why not?

4. Considering Elkanah's question in verse 8, it appears he didn't quite grasp Hannah's grief. Name several reasons why this loving husband didn't fully understand her suffering. Don't allow yourself to say, "Men are clueless." Dig deeper for how he contributed to Hannah's dilemma.

5. Draw a vertical line in the middle of a sheet of an easel pad or whiteboard. At the top of the left side print the words, "Hannah's Blessings." At the top of the right side print, "Hannah's Banes." (Banes are problems or distresses.) In spite of Hannah's desire and circumstances, what were the blessings in her life? List them on the chart. Then list the problems she faced. How could Hannah use both the blessings and banes to bolster her belief in an unfulfilled dream? How could she let these pros and cons destroy her desires?

Behind the Scenes

THE BLESSING OF BARRENNESS

Sons are a heritage from the LORD, children a reward from him. Like arrows in the hands of a warrior are sons born in one's youth. Blessed is the man whose quiver is full of them.

— Psalm 127:3–5

The psalmist wrote these words as a celebration of children, a reflection of his gratitude for family, one of God's many blessings. Unfortunately, the Israelites turned this sentiment into a painful "if-then" proposition. If children were a reward and a blessing, then infertility was a punishment and a curse. And it most likely was the barren woman's fault.

In Old Testament times childlessness named a woman a failure, an embarrassment to her husband, and a financial burden. Children played an important role in the society's social structure, providing a source of labor for families and care for old and infirm parents. Consequently, ancient Middle Eastern custom obligated an infertile wife to offer a servant girl to her husband for sexual relations and childbearing. By law a husband could even divorce a barren wife, and friends and families encouraged him to replace her with an heir-producing female.

For an Israelite wife, infertility meant a soul filled with shame.

On the other hand, Hannah's barrenness placed her in good company, along with the foremothers of her nation. Abram's wife Sarai (Genesis 11:30), Isaac's wife Rebekah (Genesis 25:21), and Jacob's wife Rachel (Genesis 29:31) all suffered the humiliation of childlessness. In these incidents God honored the woman's deep-seated dream, mastered a miracle according to his timing and purpose, and opened her womb. Even more, each of these once barren women has been immortally revered by the Jews. The Lord used their infertility to prove his care, power, and sovereignty over a nation. He turned barrenness into a blessing.

Unfortunately, at this point in Hannah's story, the pain of the present overshadows the hope of the past. She's yet to discover the blessing hidden in her barrenness.

— Judith Couchman

HANNAH — *Entrusting Your Dreams to God*

DESCRIBING THE DESIRE WITHIN

What is the object of your desire? The unfulfilled longing tucked inside you? Describing it to friends can unburden, encourage, and stimulate you to pursue it, even if circumstances make it look like the impossible dream.

1. Though Hannah lived centuries ago, most of us understand what it feels like to manage unfulfilled longings. What elements of Hannah's story still figure into the lives of contemporary women who pursue a dream or struggle to keep their hope alive?

2. According to Psalm 37:4, God "will give you the desires of your heart." Do you think this means: (a) God will give you whatever you desire; (b) he will place a specific desire in your heart and then fulfill it; or (c) he will fulfill some desires and not others? Explain your response.

3. How can you determine if an object of desire is God-inspired or self-motivated?

4. For a woman pursuing a God-inspired desire, what obstacles does she face? Write or draw a picture of these obstacles on a whiteboard or easel pad so the entire group can see it. (For example, a financial barrier could be drawn as a large dollar bill. Or an education barrier could be sketched as a schoolhouse.) Think through the personal, relational, spiritual, practical, and emotional barriers. What positive and negative choices can a woman make as she faces these obstacles? Write or draw them on the board too.

5. Sometimes it can seem like God is the obstacle to our dreams coming true. For example, he placed in Hannah's heart the desire for a child, then withheld it. How can we make sense of this seeming contradiction?

6. A challenging aspect of daring to dream is that our heartfelt desire may not come true. Or it may not materialize during our lifetime. For example, a child may not accept Christ until after a parent dies. Or some ministries reach their pinnacle after the founder retires. How do you feel about this? How can you remain faithful to God, not knowing whether your dream will come true? Why would faithfulness matter?

7. What is the dream in your heart? Describe it to the group, or read the description you wrote in the Setting the Stage section titled, "What Do You Want?" Only share what feels comfortable to you.

8. Even without this dream, what blessings exist in your life? Share a few with the group. How can you enjoy these blessings this week?

God does plant dreams in our souls, but his process of fulfilling them can be mysterious. At times he grants a desire immediately, though we've barely uttered it. Sometimes we wait faith-testing years for its fulfillment. Sometimes a dream may not materialize until after we've left the earth. But be encouraged. Our gift-giving Father does know about, care about, and fulfill his children's desires. And he delights in our gift-receiving joy.

In the meantime, as he did with Hannah, he may ask us to wait. Though we feel the unmet longing within, we can count our blessings and appreciate today, even though we've not yet received the object of our desire.

Prayer Matters

GATHERING UP HEARTS AND HOPE

Wrap up today's Bible study with honest and hopeful prayer. Form a circle and ask each group member to read aloud a verse from Psalm 20:1–7 below, affirming one another's heartfelt desires.

After the group reading, join hands, gather up your hearts, and say one-sentence prayers, with each woman expressing the dream she carries within. Ask one participant to close in a brief prayer of gratitude to God for his already apparent goodness in your lives.

> *May the LORD answer you when you are in distress; may the name of the*
> *God of Jacob protect you.*
> *May he send you help from the sanctuary and grant you support from Zion.*
> *May he remember all your sacrifices and accept your burnt offerings.*
> *May he give you the desire of your heart and make all your plans succeed.*
> *We will shout for joy when you are victorious and will lift up our banners in*
> *the name of our God. May the LORD grant all your requests.*
> *Now I know that the LORD saves his anointed; he answers him from his holy*
> *heaven with the saving power of his right hand.*
> *Some trust in chariots and some in horses, but we trust in the name of the*
> *LORD our God.*

After Hours

KEEP THE DREAM ALIVE

This week step toward your object of desire by completing one or both of the following activities. Dare to believe that when you seek him first, God wants to fulfill the desires of your heart.

With a friend: With a group member, interview a woman who, like Hannah, struggled as she waited for God to fulfill her desire. If you can, select a woman whose dream was similar to yours. Treat her to lunch and ask to glean her wisdom. For example:

- How did she feel while waiting for this dream to come true?
- How did she manage her attitudes and emotions?
- What positive steps did she take toward her dream?
- What is the silliest thing she did during this time? The wisest?
- In hindsight, what does she think should have been done differently?
- How is her fulfilled dream similar and different than what she expected?
- If she could offer you only one morsel of wisdom, what would it be?

After the lunch debrief with your friend. What are the most important principles to remember from this conversation? How can you integrate this wisdom into your lives?

On your own: Review the entry you wrote for Setting the Stage. Using the following verses and others that inspire you, turn your lament into a proclamation of God's desire to fulfill your dream. Use Psalm 37:1–7, Proverbs 3:5–6, or Matthew 6:33–34 to write statements like, "I will trust in the Lord and enjoy his 'safe pasture' as I wait for my desire. For me, his safe pastures are _____." Or, "If I seek first God's kingdom and his righteousness, my desire to _____ may be given to me as well."

Words to Remember

DAILY LOVE AND TRUST

Let the morning bring me word of your unfailing love,

for I have put my trust in you.

Show me the way I should go,

for to you I lift up my soul.

— Psalm 143:8

A Matter of the Heart

*Before God changes
circumstances, he changes us.*

*H*alf hidden in the folds of the temple's curtains, Eli sat on a chair by the doorpost and watched the young woman enter and stumble to the floor.

The old priest sighed. *She's probably drunk,* he thought. *Another one of the women who desecrate the temple with drinking and loose morals.* Recently he'd heard that the women who served at the entrance to the Tent of Meeting were sleeping with his sons. Only God knows how many more women — those from the world outside — slipped in to sin with men visiting the temple. And what about the people who didn't visit the temple at all? *We are a decaying nation,* he reminded himself. *Israel is in trouble.*

Eli observed the woman for awhile, then muttered under his breath, "Lord, how long do I have to put up with this? I'm weary from cleaning up the spiritual mess around here. When will it all change?"

Eli tilted his head as if listening for an answer, but heard nothing.

"I know, I know," the priest said in response to the silence. "I'm the one who guards the sanctity of your house. And through the years I've cherished that honor. But I'm old. These creaky bones don't move like they used to." He rose stiffly from the chair and shuffled toward the figure on the floor. "I need help, and I can't count on my wicked sons for that!"

As Eli moved closer, he noticed the woman's lips moving without sound. Feeling frustrated and judgmental, he *tsk-tsked* to himself about such irreverence. Then he cleared his throat and stomped the floor with his cane.

"Woman, this is a holy place," he said, raising his voice but keeping some distance from her. "You blaspheme the Lord by coming in here drunk. Get rid of your wine!"

The woman's body jerked slightly, as if startled by the visitor. The priest watched as she gathered herself up, blotted her cheeks with a sleeve, and looked at him. Though puffy and red-eyed from crying, her face had a unique beauty, her demeanor a gentleness he hadn't expected.

Taken aback, Eli stared at her a moment. The woman spoke before the priest could think of something more to say.

"Oh, no, my lord. I'm a woman who is deeply troubled. I haven't been drinking; I was pouring out my soul to the Lord. I've been praying in deep grief and anguish. Back home in Ephraim I've spent many hours in prayer before the Lord." She stopped, catching a sob in her throat. Her eyes filled with tears.

Eli's face softened as she cried quietly. He wondered what would cause this woman so much pain. What would compel her to spend hours in prayer? To prostrate, even humiliate, herself in the temple this way?

"Please, don't take me for a wicked woman," she begged. "I only desire the Lord's blessing."

Moved by the woman's sincerity, Eli said gently, "I can see that you're a good woman, dedicated to the Lord. Surely he will bless you. Go home in peace, and may the God of Israel answer your prayers."

"Oh, thank you," she whispered, impulsively stepping forward, but then pulling back, as if remembering their propriety. Flustered, she only repeated "Thank you!" and walked quickly toward the doorpost.

Oh, Lord, thought Eli. *So many of your people don't care about following you. But here is someone who truly prays. Maybe because of this woman, there's hope for us yet . . .*

Setting the Stage

WHAT MOTIVATES YOU?

When you tackle a project, what typically motivates you? Before this week's group session privately review the list below and check the motivations that apply to you. If needed, add motives that aren't listed.

We're all a mixtures of motives, so you'll probably check off what you consider both "good" and "bad" motivators. As you pursue your dream, the Holy Spirit can lovingly help you align your desires with God's will. So before you begin, ask him to help you recognize and sort out personal motives for pursuing your dream.

❏ Control	❏ Obedience	❏ Rewards
❏ Excellence	❏ Power	❏ Self-satisfaction
❏ Fear	❏ Skill	❏ Skill development
❏ Fun	❏ Punishment	❏ Success
❏ Giving	❏ Recognition	❏ Task completion
❏ Love	❏ Relationships	❏ Teamwork
❏ Money	❏ Respect	❏ Winning
❏ Other:	*Alignment*	

Which of these motivations would honor God as you pursue the desire of your heart? Circle them. Which would not be God honoring? Draw a line through them.

Spend time journaling, praying, and listening to the Spirit about how to fulfill your dream with motives that please and glorify God.

Discussing Hannah's Story

TRANSFORMED IN THE TEMPLE

When Hannah visited the temple with Elkanah, her despair deepened when she prostrated herself before God and prayed. Even Eli the priest, who'd heard the woes of countless countrymen, recognized her as a woman who especially needed God's touch.

Perhaps in the temple Hannah did feel her Maker's presence, for something or someone in that holy place transformed her.

Before you begin the discussion, read the Bible text, 1 Samuel 1:9–20.

1. Verse 10 says, "In bitterness of soul Hannah wept much and prayed to the LORD." With a partner write the heart-wrenching words an agonizing Hannah may have said to God before she made her vow to him. (Remember that, like us, Hannah was a real woman who spoke honestly to God.) Then as a group take turns reading these prayers aloud.

2. Read Hannah's vow in verse 11. Note the words she used to describe the Lord and herself. What does Hannah's choice of words reveal about her relationship with God? Is this the same attitude of the woman of verses 7 and 10? Why or why not?

3. Read the Behind the Scenes section, "A Question of Motives," on page 30. It presents several reasons why Hannah dedicated her unborn child to God. Which motive(s) do you agree with? Why? Would you add other possible motives to the list? If so, what are they?

4. In verses 12–18a, how would you describe Hannah's attitude as she responds to Eli the priest? Why would she desire favor with him (verse 18a)?

5. When Hannah left the temple she "ate something, and her face was no longer downcast" (verse 18b). What do you think made the difference in her actions and appearance? Explore more than one possibility.

6. "In the course of time" Hannah gave birth to a son, Samuel. Why do you think God waited until after this particular temple visit to give her a child?

Behind the Scenes

A QUESTION OF MOTIVES

Why did Hannah offer her unborn son to God? Through the years Old Testament scholars, Bible teachers, and authors have suggested motives. Here is a sampling of recent opinions:

- *Contributing to God's service.* "Hannah no doubt valued the love of her husband, but believed she could contribute more to the cause of God's kingdom by raising a child to serve God. . . . Hannah may have been deeply concerned about the apostasy of God's people and their need for dedicated, spiritual leaders. A strong desire to be used of God and to that end could have motivated and sustained

Hannah." — Diane Brummel Bloem, *Growing Godly: A Woman's Workshop on Bible Women*

- *Gaining the blessing of firstfruits.* "In Israel one gave the firstfruits of animals and of the harvest to Yahweh, probably in hopes of receiving in return the blessing of continued fertility. If Hannah's offer to dedicate her firstborn to Yahweh can be seen in this light . . . she 'offers up' her firstborn to Yahweh in hopes of receiving more children in return. The priest Eli operates within the same frame of reference, and after Samuel's birth and dedication to his temple, habitually blesses Elkanah this way (1 Samuel 2:20)." — Jo Ann Hackett, *The Women's Bible Commentary*

- *Giving the gift of gratitude.* "God's remembrance is not a matter of recalling to mind but of paying special attention to or lavishing special care on someone. Hannah recognizes that children are always a gift of God (Psalm 8:4). If he will 'give' her a son, in gratitude she will 'give' him back to the Lord (Exodus 22:29)." — Ronald F. Youngblood, *NIV Bible Commentary*

- *Securing a position in society.* "This vow in itself is telling: far from wanting a child for emotional comfort, she is offering to forgo the pleasure of having him with her while he is growing up. She seems to simply want to *give birth* to a son. At that point her societal position will be secure, even though she would still live without children." — Jo Ann Hackett, *The Women's Bible Commentary*

- *Surrendering to God's will.* "Hannah moved from wanting a child for personal reasons to desiring God's purposes fulfilled through her. Flawed and weary and wracked with pain, she turned from her own way and handed the situation back to God. It's not evident what happened between the vow and her departure, but it's apparent that when Hannah loosened her grip, she received from God." — Judith Couchman, *His Gentle Voice*

FIRST THINGS FIRST

When we finally recognize or articulate the dream within us, it's common to push the fast-forward button and rush headlong into pursuing it. And our intentions can be good: the need is great; time seems to be passing quickly; people are urging us onward; we see other "dreamers" galloping ahead of us and we want to catch up.

But God may have other plans. Before we jump headlong into the dream (or even as we start to pursue it) he wants to take care of "first things first." He may guide us through a change process, transforming us before he alters our circumstances. Like Hannah, he might want us to mold our desires to reflect his purpose in the world. Or he may want to free us from a destructive habit or attitude. Or he could deepen us spiritually before we wade into new challenges. Whatever the case, we're stepping closer to our dreams when we cooperate with rather than fight this process.

1. What motivates you toward the desire in your heart? Share some of your responses in "What Motivates You?" the Setting the Stage section on page 27. (If most of the group didn't have time to complete this section before the meeting, allow a few minutes to do it now.)

2. How can you determine if your motives are from God? Does a person need "good" motives to receive from God? Explain your answer, giving examples from Scripture or your own experience.

3. As mentioned earlier, God may want to transform us before he alters our circumstances and fulfills a dream. In addition to motives, what other changes might he want to make?

4. In her book *Living a Purpose-Full Life*, author Jan Johnson explains, "In order for God to have freedom to work his purposes in us, we need to offer him our destructive attitudes and motives." Otherwise, "we will pursue our purposes with a self-serving agenda." She mentions the "voices in our heads" that lead to self-promotion, listed below. Review the list, and next to each self-focused feeling or attitude suggest the quality that God wants to replace it with. For example, he wants to replace despair with _____. If a Scripture comes to anyone's mind that mentions the God-given quality, look it up and read it together.

- despair

- ambition

- fear

- self-protection

- conflict

- self-justification

- self-doubt

5. As we experience God's change process — especially while we're waiting for a dream to come true — how can we learn to view it as God's kindness rather than his punishment? For example, if he focuses on our problem with pride or anger, how can we view this as his goodness toward us?

6. If God passes us through a change process, how can we entrust our dreams to him during this time?

God works changes in us for our good. So we can be free from what binds us. So we can truly enjoy his gifts to us. So we will follow him and not our own way. As he molds us in his loving hands, we can entrust our dreams to him. He has not forgotten them. He is preparing us for their fulfillment.

Prayer Matters

A REQUEST FOR REVELATION

As you close today, use the prayer of Clement of Rome, who lived around the turn of the second century, to quietly ask God to reveal his truth to your hearts. Each woman can pray his words silently, then spend a few minutes asking the Lord to reveal the motives, attitudes, and actions that he wants to lovingly change while she waits for her dream. Designate a group member to close in prayer.

O God Almighty, Father of our Lord Jesus Christ, we pray thee, to be grounded and settled in thy truth by the coming down of the Holy Spirit into our hearts.

That which we know not, do thou reveal; that which is wanting in us, do thou fill up; that which we know, do thou confirm; and keep us blameless in thy service, through the same Jesus Christ our Lord. Amen.

After Hours

DARE TO BE BETTER

When the Lord highlights personal qualities that need to change, we can do our part to facilitate the process. These suggestions can ease you into action, helping you to appreciate rather than resist his work.

With a friend: With another "dreamer" you trust, plan to meet at least once a month to encourage each other to make the changes God asks of you. Let these "Dare to Be Better" sessions be a safe place to laugh and lament, prod and pray together as you work toward change. For example, in the first session you can share your dreams. In the second, you could discuss the changes God asks of you. In another session you might set goals for personal change. Then in future sessions, share your progress, successes, and failures, offering hope and encouragement to each other.

On your own: Use a Bible concordance to conduct a word study on a habit, action, attitude, or quality that you want to change. In the concordance look up a word that represents your need and note its biblical references. Then find these verses in the Bible and write out the ones that fit your concern. (For example, if you are struggling to forgive someone who has hurt you, find and look up verses on mercy, grace, and forgiveness.) What is the overall message of these Scriptures? How can you apply the principles in these verses to your life?

AN INSIDE SEARCH

Search me, O God, and know my heart;

test me and know my anxious thoughts.

See if there is any offensive way in me,

and lead me in the way everlasting.

— Psalm 139:23–24

A Promise Kept

A vow to the Creator
is a pledge to remember.

*E*lkanah's headdress fluttered in the wind as he crossed a field under the descending sun. With each hardy step the furrows in his brow seemed to relax a bit more, and his lips parted into a faint smile.

"Time for dinner," he said to his old tagalong dog, who jumped and barked at the sound of *dinner.* "Time to see my beautiful Hannah." The dog ran ahead of Elkanah for a while, missing that his master's anticipation wasn't just about food. Elkanah's smile broadened.

"Silly old dog," Elkanah shouted after him. "You don't know how fortunate you are! Can't do much work, but you still eat well. You are blessed!"

Blessed like me, thought Elkanah as he caught sight of his house. *Blessed to come home to such a happy wife.* These past few years had been the best of his life. The moment Hannah knew she was pregnant, their marriage improved remarkably. Hannah was joyous and more beautiful than ever before. She also was more accessible, not just to him, but to everyone in the household. She wasn't spending hours crying and praying and begging God for a child. She'd rejoined the family.

"Thank you, Yahweh, for giving Hannah back to me," he said, casting a look skyward. "A man does need his wife."

Elkanah and his raggedy dog sprinted the last yards to his house. As he passed by Peninnah and her daughters, stirring and pounding and baking their dinner, he patted them each on the arm. But his eyes searched for Hannah.

"Where is she?" he asked, not needing to mention her name.

"Upstairs with the child," Peninnah huffed, not looking up from the steaming pot before her. "She should be with us!"

Elkanah ignored Peninnah's criticism and stepped into his bedroom, just as Hannah laid their toddler on a mat to sleep.

"Hannah?"

"Shh, Samuel is asleep," she whispered to her husband, who kneeled beside the sleeping child with her. With one arm around his wife and the other free to stroke his son's back, Elkanah sighed. It was all too good to be true. And suddenly he was reminded, once again, that all too soon it would end. He looked down at his wife, fixed on her boy's every breath, and wondered if she'd survive giving up this beloved child.

Hannah pulled him out of the dim room. "Elkanah, come to dinner, and I'll tell you what Samuel did today," she said. He relaxed as Hannah chattered about their son and handed him plates of food. Her face glowed, more radiant than the embers of their evening fire.

"Samuel did the funniest thing today," she began, but Elkanah didn't hear. He could only think of his wife's vow — their vow — that this son would be taken to the temple and left there for life. *Yet each day she grows more attached to him,* he thought. *To give him up will kill her . . . kill us. Lord, please help Hannah to be strong. Please help us all.*

"Elkanah, are you listening?" asked Hannah, leaning into his face with a quizzical look.

"Yes, dear," he said, snapping back to a family sitting at the table, staring at him. "And I'm ready to eat. But first, let's pray. We need God's blessing for all we have, and for all that is to come."

Setting the Stage

THE ROAD TO COMMITMENT

Choosing to pursue a dream isn't an all-at-once decision. It's usually a process of unearthing your feelings, consulting God about it, and taking incremental steps toward commitment. Sometime before this week's session, consider these steps toward the pursuit of a dream, which aren't always taken in this order.

Feeling the desire. Recognizing the stirring within and listening to it.
Naming the dream. Describing the desire to yourself and others.
Praying about it. Seeking God as to whether the dream is his will.
Exploring the options. Looking at ways to fulfill the dream.

HANNAH — *Entrusting Your Dreams to God*

Counting the cost. Determining the dream's risk and practical aspects.
Creating a plan. Planning how to pursue and develop the dream.
Accepting God's timing. Waiting for the Lord's movement.
Choosing to commit. Deciding to move ahead with the dream.

Are there other steps you'd add to this process? If so, add them here:

Which steps have you taken toward pursuing your dream? Check them. At which step are you now? Circle it. Spend time exploring how, with God's help, you can move to the next step.

Discussing Hannah's Story

THE POWER OF A PLEDGE

Scripture doesn't explicitly record how Hannah felt during the years she cuddled and nursed her baby at home. But one can imagine. As he grew, Samuel's smile, laughter through their home, and spontaneous expressions of love must have tugged at her mother heart. Giving up her beloved boy would be painful and profound. So what kept her on course, committed to a promise uttered years before?

Before you begin the discussion, read the Bible text, 1 Samuel 1:21–28; 2:11.

1. Read Hannah's request to her husband in verses 21–22. Why would Hannah want to stay home instead of traveling to the temple?

2. How did Elkanah's response in 1 Samuel 1:23 differ from his reply in 1 Samuel 1:8? Why would this be?

3. In the Behind the Scenes section, "Promises, Promises," on page 41, read about the making and breaking of vows in Scripture, especially pledges made to God. Why do you think Elkanah supported his wife's vow to the Lord?

4. As Hannah nurtured her young son, how might she have justified defaulting on her promise to God? Name several reasons.

5. In verses 24–28, Hannah offered a ceremonial sacrifice to the Lord, then sacrificed again by keeping her vow to him. With these actions, what character qualities did she exhibit? How had she grown since her last encounter with Eli?

Behind the Scenes

PROMISES, PROMISES

When Hannah promised her son to God, she entered into a vow with the Creator. One Bible commentator describes a vow as "a solemn promise or pledge that binds a person to perform a specified act or to behave in a certain manner." In the Old and New Testaments a vow constituted a *voluntary* pledge made to God, not to a person or organization. It expressed unusual devotion, and both the vow-maker and the Lord took it seriously.

Scripture offers insight to the nature of vow-making in Hannah's culture:

- The promise expected God's favor in return (Genesis 28:20).

- A vow could be an expression of thanksgiving for God's blessings (Psalm 116:12–19).

- A vow could be part of everyday devotion or annual festivals (Psalm 61:8; 1 Samuel 1:21).

- It was paid in the congregation at the tabernacle or temple (Deuteronomy 12:6, 11; Psalm 22:25).

- Though voluntary, a vow was to be fulfilled (Deuteronomy 23:21–23).

- Careful consideration should precede a vow (Proverbs 20:25).

- A vow should align with what pleased God (Leviticus 27:9–27).

- A deceptive vow brought a curse (Malachi 1:14).

In Hannah's culture a limit was placed on women who made vows (Numbers 30:3–9). Husbands and fathers were legally responsible for their wives and children and could overrule vows made by those in their guardianship.

— Judith Couchman

FACTORS FOR FAITHFULNESS

Hannah was committed to her dream's fulfillment due to a deep personal desire, but also because of her vow to God. What keeps you committed to waiting for your dream? What will keep you faithful once it arrives? Exploring these questions could help form your attitude about faithfulness in the future.

1. As a group review the suggested steps toward commitment in the Setting the Stage section, "The Road to Commitment," on page 38. In regard to your dream, which step are you on? Share your answer with the group.

2. Wherever you are on the journey, what will motivate you to keep working toward and asking God for your dream? What do you think will keep you committed to the dream when it's fulfilled? List the group's responses in two separate columns on a whiteboard or easel pad so everyone can see them. Title them "Dream Desired" and "Dream Fulfilled." Which of these "commitment factors" would be the most crucial to emphasize? Why? As a group circle three factors in each column.

3. Why are we inclined to make promises to God when we ask him for something?

4. Do you think it's necessary to make promises to God for him to fulfill a dream? Why or why not? When would it be appropriate to make a vow to God in regard to your dream?

5. How can we guard against making impulsive or unkept promises to God? If we have offered him broken promises, what can we do?

With or without our promises, with or without our dreams, most of all God cares about our faithfulness to him. As we walk the "road to commitment" toward our heart's desire, we're to focus on our relationship with him. Following him is a promise worth keeping for a lifetime.

Prayer Matters

A STEADFAST HEART

Before your prayer time, pass out an index card to each group member. Write the following unfinished sentence on a whiteboard or easel pad and request that each woman complete it by writing her "answer" on the card. The responses can be anonymous.

"As I entrust God with my dreams, I want to be faithful to _____ _____."

The responses will be unique to each individual, but overall they could include actions like "spend time with God in his Word," "handle my finances honorably," "grow more trustworthy in my friendships," or "take time to pray each day."

Collect the cards and give them to one person who will read them to the group. Afterwards, read in unison this prayer by Thomas á Kempis, written in the fourteenth or fifteenth century.

Give us, O Lord, steadfast hearts that cannot be dragged down by false loves; give us courageous hearts that cannot be worn down by trouble; give us righteous hearts that cannot be sidetracked by unholy or unworthy goals.

Give to us also, our Lord and God, understanding to know you, diligence to look for you, wisdom to recognize you, and a faithfulness that will bring us to see you face-to-face. Amen.

After Hours

BE A PROMISE KEEPER

Following through on promises doesn't need to be difficult. It can be fun and rewarding. Try these ideas for feeling the joy of being a promise keeper.

With a friend: Meet for coffee to list a few things you each promised to do for someone, but didn't. Your lists could include activities such as returning a book, writing a letter, going to a special event, completing a chore, taking a child to the zoo, or visiting someone in a nursing home. During the next month follow through on your promise, no matter how old it is.

You may want to send a card ahead of time, stating why and when you're fulfilling the promise. Check in with your promise-keeping partner to relive the fun of surprising someone with an almost forgotten promise.

On your own: Start a promise-keeping chain. Purchase a card that's blank on the inside and write this message:

I am starting a promise-keeping chain. With this card I promise to *(fill in the promise)* for you by *(fill in the date or time period)*. Please keep the chain going. Send a promise card to a friend and ask her/him to send a promise card, too. Just think about how many people will be touched by the joy of a promise kept!

Give the card to a friend, and be sure to keep your promise!

Words to Remember

EVERYDAY PRAISE

Then will I ever sing praise to your name
and fulfill my vows day after day.

— Psalm 61:8

The Source of Strength

The Lord deserves honor
for dreams come true.

*H*annah kissed Samuel one last time and placed her child's chubby fingers in Eli's wrinkled palm. When the boy and the old man clasped hands, Hannah waited for her heart to tear in two. By giving up Samuel, she was losing at least half, if not all, of her soul.

Instead, she felt inexplicably calm.

Am I not a good mother? Hannah questioned herself. *I've nursed and cherished this child. Why aren't I soaked with tears?* Samuel's voice interrupted her thoughts before she could find an answer.

"Bye, bye, Mama," said the boy, not old enough to grasp that this was a permanent parting. "I will be good for Eli today."

"Bye, bye, my dear son," she echoed and stepped away to lean on her husband's arm. Together they watched as their child, curious and chattering, walked away with the pensive priest. Hannah memorized every step and movement.

When Samuel's small body disappeared behind a door, Elkanah pulled Hannah to his chest to comfort her, as he'd done countless times before. Hannah breathed from deep within, and for a few moments husband and wife held each other without words.

Then Hannah whispered, "Elkanah, I want to pray. I need to spend time with God."

"Do what you feel is best," he replied. "I'll wait for you outside."

As Hannah kneeled to pray, not far from the doorpost where Eli had sat a few years ago, she waited again for tears to well up. Instead, she felt surprised by the joy within — a spurt at first, then a splattering fountain, then a rushing sensation so strong, she stood to her feet. Filled with the presence of God, she clapped her hands and sang:

My heart rejoices in the LORD; in the LORD my horn is lifted high.
My mouth boasts over my enemies, for I delight in your deliverance.
There is no one holy like the LORD; there is no one besides you;
*   there is no Rock like our God.*

Hannah stopped for a moment. Was anyone watching her? Would they think she'd gone mad? After all, she'd just relinquished her son. But this feeling, this desire to praise God, moved beyond her control. It rushed up again, this time with overwhelming gratitude. So she lifted her hands and praised. She praised not for herself alone, but for Israel, for all humanity. What she'd been taught all her life — about God's goodness and care of his people — sprang up new in her heart.

She who was barren has borne seven children, but she who has had many
*   sons pines away.*
The LORD brings death and makes alive; he brings down to the grave and
*   raises up.*
The LORD sends poverty and wealth; he humbles and he exalts.
He raises the poor from the dust and lifts the needy from the ash heap; he
*   seats them with princes and has them inherit a throne of honor.*

When the song ended Hannah sat quietly before the Lord, letting the stirring within subside. "Lord, I know that later I'll miss Samuel terribly. And the tears will come," she admitted. "But thank you for getting me through this part, for blessing me with your peace and joy." Then tired but calm, she rose to find her husband.

Setting the Stage

A DREAMER'S GUIDE TO PRAYER

In his book, *Prayer: Finding the Heart's True Home*, Richard Foster describes the types of prayers we utter while growing in our relationship with God. Some of these prayers include:

- *Simple Prayer.* "Our needs, our wants, our concerns dominate the prayer experience."

- *Prayer of the Forsaken.* "Here we experience real spiritual desolation. We feel abandoned by friends, spouse, and God."

- *The Prayer of Relinquishment.* "We begin to enter into a grace-filled releasing of our will and a flowing into the will of the Father. It is the Prayer of Relinquishment that moves us from the struggling to the releasing."

- *Covenant Prayer.* "At the altar of Covenant Prayer we vow unswerving allegiance; we make high resolves; we promise holy obedience."

- *The Prayer of Adoration.* "Adoration is the spontaneous yearning of the heart to worship, honor, magnify, and bless God."

Foster's descriptions mirror the kind of pleas and praises Hannah may have uttered to God, and the prayers we can offer while learning to entrust him with our dreams. We may pray one kind of prayer for days or months or years.

Before attending group discussion, in this section "sample" each type of prayer as it relates to your heart's desire. After each of Foster's descriptions write a corresponding one-sentence prayer that expresses your feelings about your dream. For example, you can begin the Simple Prayer with "Lord, I want ..." The Covenant Prayer can start with "Lord, I promise to ..." If you're not ready to pray a certain type of prayer, you can write, "God, someday I would like to offer a Prayer of Relinquishment that says ..."

In relationship to your dream, what type of prayer are you ready to pray these days? Each day this week, offer that "category" of prayer to God.

Discussing Hannah's Story

A TIME FOR ADORATION

Hannah offers a prayer to God filled with praise and thanksgiving. Bible scholars say her prayer probably wasn't original, but drawn from traditional songs often sung by Jewish worshipers.

However Hannah's words originated, she continued a life of prayer by acknowledging God as the source of strength and blessings — even though she'd just left her child in the temple.

Before you begin the discussion, read the Bible text, 1 Samuel 2:1–10.

1. During Hannah's quest for a child, she offered repeated prayers to the Lord. Review Richard Foster's types/definitions of prayer in the Setting the Stage section, "A Dreamer's Guide to Prayer," on page 47. When did Hannah express each one of these prayers to God? Why was each type of prayer appropriate at that point?

2. Just prior to Hannah's Prayer of Adoration she surrendered her only son to Eli. Why was she able to worship instead of weep?

3. In the Behind the Scenes section on page 51 read about "Hannah's Classic Prayer" and two significant names she ascribed to the Lord. Then in the space below list three other names in verses 2–3 that she called him. Why would each of these characteristics of God be meaningful to Hannah?

4. Early in her prayer Hannah presented groupings of "opposites" to emphasize contrast. For example, in verse 4 she contrasted warriors with stumblers. On the whiteboard or easel pad list these pairs in verses 4–9. What is the overall message Hannah communicated through these contrasts? Why would she want to present this message?

5. Scholars suggest that the references to "the king" were added to Hannah's prayer later, since at that time Israel was ruled by judges. Why would these references be added by the author (whom many suggest to be Samuel) or a later writer?

HANNAH – *Entrusting Your Dreams to God*

Behind the Scenes

HANNAH'S CLASSIC PRAYER

The prayer of the mother of Samuel is regarded as one of the most outstanding prayers of the Bible. In it she especially exulted in the greatness of God and His grace in raising up the humble and insignificant to confound the wise and mighty. This very appropriately set the tone and emphasis of the books of Samuel where this principle is constantly stressed.

Her prayers also introduced the use of two significant names of the Lord:

1. The first is "the LORD of hosts" (1 Samuel 1:11), a designation used nearly 300 times in the Old Testament. As Moses sang of the Lord as a "man of war" and Joshua saw Him as a "Commander of the army of the LORD," (Exodus 15:3; Joshua 5:14), Hannah's prayer states, "The LORD kills and makes alive" (1 Samuel 2:6), adverting to His almightiness.

2. Hannah also referred to God's king as "His anointed," (1 Samuel 2:10), a term interpreted as "Messiah" in Daniel 9:25–26, and the derivation of the name "Christ" in the New Testament. This anointing spoke of the Spirit's power by which men of God and even the Messiah performed God's service.

These two designations, "the LORD of hosts" and "His anointed," nicely introduce the books of Samuel where David is anointed [by Samuel] with the Spirit's power to serve the Lord of hosts in destroying the enemies of the Lord and setting up His kingdom.

— Stanley A. Ellisen, *Knowing God's Word*

CREDIT WHEN IT'S DUE

Growing in a relationship with God means moving beyond our desires and focusing on the Lord — not only for what he does for us but also for who he is. We can begin shifting our focus by giving him credit when credit is due.

1. At this point in pursuing your dream, which of Foster's prayers in the Setting the Stage section, "A Dreamer's Guide to Prayer," on page 47–48 do you say the most? Why? Which type of prayer would you like to learn to pray? Why?

2. It's been said, "The very act of praise releases the power of God into a set of circumstances and enables God to change them if this is his design." For what other reasons do we praise and thank God?

3. How can we learn to offer prayers of praise, even if our dream hasn't been fulfilled yet? How could praising God affect us?

4. When a dream is fulfilled, we can forget to thank and praise God for his goodness to us. Why does this happen?

5. When a dream is fulfilled, how can we remember to give God credit for it? Spend time brainstorming ways to memorialize him as the source of good gifts. For example, you could write a poem or song, create a banner or painting, keep a list of the "good gifts" that he gives to you, or make a point to give him credit during a "sharing time" at church.

Whatever the circumstances, we don't need to look far to find God's goodness toward us. Small or big, we can find joy, relief, and encouragement in remembering him as our source of strength.

Prayer Matters

THANK YOU, LORD

We can give God credit not only through praise, but also with thanksgiving. Before you leave, say brief, spontaneous prayers aloud to the Lord. First, praise him for his attributes, such as his faithfulness or longsuffering or loving-kindness. Second, thank him for specific blessings in your life.

After offering your prayers, conclude by reading together these words of thanksgiving from the *Book of Common Prayer*, composed in the eighteenth century.

> *Accept, O Lord, our thanks and praise for all that you have done for us. We thank you for the splendor of the whole creation, for the beauty of this world, for the wonder of life, and for the mystery of love.*
>
> *We thank you for the blessing of family and friends, and for the loving care which surrounds us on every side.*
>
> *We thank you for setting us at tasks which demand our best efforts, and for leading us to accomplishments which satisfy and delight us.*
>
> *We thank you also for those disappointments and failures that lead us to acknowledge our dependence on you alone....*

Grant us the gift of your Spirit, that we may know Christ and make
him known; and through him, at all times and in all places, may give
thanks to you in all things.
  Amen.

MAKE IT A PARTY

While we wait for a dream to come true — or even midst the busyness
of fulfilling it — we can overlook God's good gifts to us, especially the
things that seem "small" compared to the "big picture" we keep in mind.
Cultivating an attitude of praise and thanksgiving can change our per-
spective, helping us see that God continually loves and provides for us.

With a friend: Throw a praise party. With a few friends hang streamers,
toss confetti, use noisemakers, sing praise songs, and spend time offering prayers of adoration to God for his many blessings. You might also
work on a project, such as making a praise banner for your church, com-
posing a song, or studying one of the Bible's praise psalms.

On your own: As you work toward or live your dream, keep a praise journal. Jot down answers to prayer and other things that reflect God's
blessings in your life. Next to each entry, write a one-sentence praise or
thanksgiving to him. Later, as you look back, you can celebrate the constant (but sometimes forgotten) presence of God's goodness toward you.
To keep the pressure off, you may want to limit this activity to one week,
recording a few simple things each day. After this, you can decide if
you'd like to continue the journal for a longer period of time.

Words to Remember

REASONS TO PRAISE

I will give you thanks, for you answered me;
you have become my salvation.

        — Psalm 118:21

A Lifetime of Letting Go

*Living the dream means
learning to surrender.*

*S*amuel missed his mother.

Lying in the semidarkness late at night, he thought about her last visit to the temple. Closing his eyes, the boy envisioned Hannah's face: the lilting smile, the dancing eyes, the mouth full of kisses for his curly-haired head. Squeezing his eyes tighter and pulling the blanket to his chin, he imagined his mother's embrace. She'd held him so tight he'd almost stopped breathing, but he didn't mind. Every ounce of Hannah delighted in her son, and he knew that. He needed to know that. Living in the temple could be lonely for a boy whose father figure was an emotionally distant old priest.

So Samuel welcomed his mother's hugs, though other boys his age might have been embarrassed by the affection. Hannah's love had to last a long time — long enough to endure their many days of separation. After each glorious visit, full of simple gifts and elaborate stories of home, she'd return to their family in the hills. He'd stay behind in God's house, remembering his mother's words.

"Samuel, I love you so much, and I miss you with all my heart!" she'd exclaimed as she left, looking back over her shoulder. "Remember, you have important work to do for God, and he will watch over you while we're apart. You can trust him, Samuel. You can put your faith in him." Hannah's voice quavered, and she turned abruptly, hoping the boy hadn't detected her tears.

But Samuel had seen.

In bed he turned on his side, wiped away the trickles on his face, and watched the flickering lamp of God about to extinguish itself for the night. *God's house must be a place for tears,* he thought. In this temple Hannah had fallen to the floor, weeping and begging the Lord for a son.

"Then God gave me a miracle. He gave me you!" she'd told him many times, gently tousling his hair. During his short life Samuel had heard the story over and over, but he'd never tired of it. "Tell me again about how much you wanted to have me for a son," he had said, and Hannah had laughed, sighed deeply, and reminisced again.

Jehovah must be wonderful, thought Samuel as he rolled onto his stomach. Why else would Mama have left him in the temple at such a young age? Why else would he have spent his childhood here? Why else would she feel proud of his job serving the Lord by helping Eli?

Jehovah must love me for giving me such a mother.

Comforted, he fell asleep.

Setting the Stage

THE GLAD SURRENDER

In your group session this week you'll discover how Hannah lived her dream by learning to surrender. It's a concept we can overlook when pursuing our heart's desire. Or we may focus on an initial surrendering to God's overall will, but not the daily, step-by-step glad obedience that brings a dream to pass.

In his book, *Absolute Surrender,* the pastor and missionary Andrew Murray explained the connection between surrender to God and his blessing:

> God waits to bless us in a way beyond what we expect. From the beginning, ear has not heard nor has eye seen what God has prepared for them that wait for Him (1 Corinthians 2:9). God has prepared unheard-of things, things we never can think of — blessing, much more wonderful than we can imagine, more mighty than we can conceive. They are divine blessings. We must come at once and say, "I give myself absolutely to God, to His will, to do only what God wants." It is God who will enable us to carry out that surrender.
>
> We must also say, "I give myself absolutely to God, to let Him work in me to will and do of His good pleasure," as He has promised to do. Yes, the living God wants to work in His children in a way we cannot understand but God's Word has re-

vealed. He wants to work in us every moment of the day. God is willing to maintain our life. Only let our absolute surrender be one of simple, childlike, and unbounded trust.

After reading Murray's thoughts, prayerfully answer these questions about developing and living your dream.

- How has God initially asked you to surrender to his will as you've thought about or begun to work toward your dream?

- How will you need to surrender to him day by day as you pursue this dream?

- What obstacles might stand in the way of your daily surrender? How can you overcome them?

If you feel ready, write a prayer to God that surrenders not only your dream, but your daily pursuits to him and the timing of his blessings. If you're not ready, describe why you feel that way.

Discussing Hannah's Story

A BLESSING FOR OBEDIENCE

Once Hannah left Samuel with the old priest, she faced the emotions of living a lifetime without her son. How did she manage day to day? The Bible doesn't say. But through her yearly visits to the temple, we observe a consistently God-fearing woman. And we see that there are blessings for those who persistently obey.

Before you begin the discussion, read the Bible text, 1 Samuel 2:18–26.

1. Even though Hannah's dream of a son was fulfilled, how did she continue to practice surrender and obedience to God? See verses 18–19.

2. Verses 22–25 describe the conduct of Eli's sons in the temple. (Also see 2:12–17.) How could this state of affairs have affected Hannah's resolve to leave Samuel behind with Eli every year? What does it suggest about Hannah that she didn't try taking her son home?

3. Read about "The Little Boy Nazirite" in the following Behind the Scenes section on page 59. Consulting verse 18 and that section, what might have comforted Hannah each time she left her son behind?

4. Read Eli's words to Elkanah and Hannah in verse 20. Why would he bless them each year?

Behind the Scenes

THE LITTLE BOY NAZIRITE

A Nazirite [NAZZ uh right] was a person who took a vow to separate from certain worldly things and to consecrate himself to God (Numbers 6:1–8). Among the Hebrew people anyone could take this vow; there were no tribal restrictions as in the case of the priest. Rich or poor, man or woman, master or slave — all were free to become Nazirites.

Nazirites did not withdraw from society and live as hermits; however, they did agree to follow certain regulations for a specific period of time. While no number of days for the vow is given in the Old Testament, Jewish tradition prescribed 30 days or a double period of 60 or even triple of 90 to 100 days.

Once a person decided to make himself "holy unto the LORD" (Numbers 6:8) for some special service, he then agreed to abstain from wine. This prohibition was so strict that it included grapes, grape juice, and raisins. Perhaps this was to guard the Nazirite from being controlled by any spirit other than God's (Proverbs 20:1; Ephesians 5:17–18).

While under the Nazirite vow, a person refused to cut his hair, including shaving (Numbers 6:5). The purpose of this long hair was to serve as a visible sign of the Nazirite's consecration to the Lord (verse 7). A Nazirite also refused to touch or go near a dead body because this would make him ceremonially unclean.

Samson, Samuel, and John the Baptist were the only "Nazirites for life" recorded in the Bible. Before they were born, their vows were taken for them by their parents. While Samuel is not specifically called a Nazirite, 1 Samuel 1:11, 28 hints that he probably was. His mother, Hannah, made a vow before his birth: "No razor shall come upon his head" (1 Samuel 1:11).

The presence of many Nazirites was considered a sign of God's blessings on Israel.

— Ronald F. Youngblood, general editor,
Nelson's New Illustrated Bible Dictionary

5. Through the years Hannah gave birth to five more children (verse 21). What could this reveal about God's character?

6. Verse 26 indicates how Samuel prospered in the temple. What do you think made this possible? Suggest at least three ideas.

Sharing Your Story

THE ONGOING DREAM

1. When a dream is fulfilled, how might we still need to surrender to God? Why?

2. Based on Hannah's life and later her son's words to Saul in 1 Samuel 15:22, what is crucial in our relationship with the Lord? Why would God value this quality so highly?

3. How does a follower of God grow to understand obedience as joy rather than drudgery?

4. As we live the dream, in what ways can we practice ongoing, daily obedience to God?

5. How can we prepare for and deal with the surprises, pitfalls, and disappointments that accompany a fulfilled dream? Write three to five affirmations to remember.

6. Despite these drawbacks, how can we still rejoice in the dream's fulfillment? Suggest practical ways to keep the dream's joy alive.

Walking with God requires obedience. So does living our dream. It is obedience that guides, protects, and blesses us. It also enables us to wholeheartedly carry out our work in the world.

"I will always obey your law, for ever and ever," wrote the psalmist. "I will walk about in freedom, for I have sought out your precepts" (Psalm 119:44–45). Obedience sets us free to be all God created us to be.

Prayer Matters

SPEAK, LORD

Conclude this session by practicing listening prayer. Ask one woman to read the following eighteenth-century prayer by the poet Christina Rossetti. Then sit in silence, waiting for God to speak to you individually about the obedience he asks of you. Afterward you might want to share the Lord's impressions with the group. The group's leader can close the prayer time by thanking God for his guidance.

> *Speak, Lord, for thy servant heareth. Grant us ears to hear, eyes to see, wills to obey, hearts to love; then declare what thou wilt, reveal what thou wilt, command what thou wilt, demand what thou wilt. Amen.*

After Hours

HELP FROM OUR FRIENDS

Sometimes learning how others obeyed God can help us in our own process of ongoing surrender. To keep growing spiritually, we can benefit from the help of our friends.

With a friend: For your quiet time with God over a week, choose the life of another biblical character and read how surrender/obedience (or the lack of it) affected his or her life. You may want to study Abraham, Joshua, Ruth, Esther, Mary, or another person of interest. Then get together and compare notes on what you learned about entrusting God with your dreams.

HANNAH – *Entrusting Your Dreams to God*

On your own: If obedience sounds demanding and too difficult for you, consider meeting privately with a counselor or trusted friend to sort out and pray through your reservations. You could also read about people who obeyed God, noting their attitude and reward. What positive lessons can you derive from their lives?

Words to Remember

DISCOVER THE DELIGHT

Direct me in the path of your commands, for there I find delight.

— Psalm 119:35

A Lingering Influence

God uses our dreams to serve his purposes.

*A*s a tired Samuel packed up for a journey to Ramah, the next stop on his priestly travel itinerary, he heard a familiar voice behind him.

"Samuel, my lord, may I talk with you?"

It was David, the last son of Jesse. The one that only a few hours ago, he'd anointed as Israel's next king. Samuel, bent over a bag stuffed with goods, pulled himself up and looked into the young shepherd's rugged face.

He's barely a man and now he's a king, still dripping with the oil of anointment, thought Samuel. *He has no idea what's ahead of him.*

"Samuel, may I ask you something?"

"Yes, of course," answered the priest kindly. "It will be the first of many things you'll ask of me."

"How can I be a good king?"

Samuel nodded, pleased with the question. "I will give you the same wisdom I handed to Saul. They are words directly from Yahweh." The priest cleared his throat. "'Does the LORD delight in burnt offerings and sacrifices as much as in obeying the voice of the LORD? To obey is better than sacrifice, and to heed is better than the fat of rams.'"

Samuel paused briefly, placed his hand on David's arm, and added, "This advice is too late for Saul, but it can be a beginning for you. I came to Bethlehem to sacrifice to the Lord, and here he directed me to you. Obedience is the foundation for all of our service, David."

David looked deeper into the priest's eyes, searching for more. "But how did you learn to obey? How did you become a holy man?"

"Ah, that is an easy one to answer," replied the priest with a smile. "I learned that from my mother, Hannah. Long ago she vowed to God that if she could have a son, she'd offer him for a lifetime of service in the temple. That's how, as a very young boy, I became a Nazirite and went to live with the old priest Eli...." His voice quavered slightly and trailed off for a moment. Samuel often felt emotional when he spoke of his mother.

Then the priest finished. "My mother followed through on her promise. She believed we're to honor and obey God. But she also prayed, David. She prayed that I'd be a man who obeys and serves."

"What a wonderful heritage," said David.

"I've felt her influence every day of my life," said Samuel. "I credit her for my service to God and his people."

"But were you afraid?"

"Oh, yes. Especially the first time I heard the Lord speak to me. A little boy in the temple by himself, and I hear the voice of the Lord? Terrifying. But I remembered my mother's words and example. I knew I was to obey."

David stood silently, soaking in the words.

Samuel wondered if the soon-to-be king had understood his advice. *So handsome and vulnerable. So eager yet inexperienced. Will he recall this wisdom when he needs it?*

"So that is how I serve?" the young man asked, as if reassuring himself.

"Yes, God calls us to serve others for his purposes," said Samuel, picking up his parcel. "If you'll listen, that's how he'll direct you. That's how he guides me. And that's how he used my mother."

"Thank you," David said.

"Live long, serve well, my new king," Samuel replied, turning to leave. "And remember the story of Hannah."

Setting the Stage

TWO-HANDED BLESSINGS

"God gives us two hands — one to receive with and one to give with," writes the evangelist Billy Graham. "We are not cisterns made for hoarding; we are channels made for sharing." Graham's wisdom applies to our dreams. Though we enjoy the blessing of a dream come true, God desires that we use it for his redemptive purposes in people's lives.

Before this week's session, think about the people who can be influenced through your dream. Consider these questions:

- Who can be influenced by the fulfillment of your dream?

- How, specifically, can you share God's redemption with them?

- What personal qualities and strengths can help you minister to these people?

- How can you better prepare for service?

- How might your fulfilled desire influence people even after your lifetime?

As a reminder of how you might influence others, write this session's "Words to Remember" verse on an index card. On the flip side, write a sentence about how you'd like to serve others through your dream. Tuck the card in your Bible as a bookmark and then periodically review it for encouragement.

Discussing Hannah's Story

LIKE MOTHER, LIKE SON

Like mother, like son. We use this cliché to acknowledge how children often mimic the attitudes and lifestyles of their parents. Applied to Hannah and her son, it's also a compliment. In Samuel's first encounter with

God, he practices the obedience of his mother, even though the task ahead looks daunting. Though they live apart, Hannah's many prayers and sacrifices have reached her son.

Before you begin the discussion, read the Bible text, 1 Samuel 3.

1. The beginning of chapter 3 claims that the Lord rarely spoke to or appeared to people during this era. Why would he choose to speak to Samuel?

2. How might Eli have felt when he realized the Lord was speaking to Samuel (verse 8)? Why would he encourage Samuel to hear from God, though Eli was the resident priest?

3. What does observing Samuel's responses in verses 11–18 tell you about him? In what ways does he mirror his mother's character?

4. In verse 18 why would Eli respond the way he did?

5. According to verses 19–21, how did God continue to honor Hannah through her son?

6. Read about Samuel's influence on Israel in the following Behind the Scenes section, "The Making of a Leader." Do you think that when Hannah made her vow, she thought her son would become the nation's leader? Why or why not?

Behind the Scenes

THE MAKING OF A LEADER

Even in ancient Israel godly leaders were hard to find. Samuel, one of the nation's greatest leaders, was one of a few. His life reflects the story of an intimate God-with-man relationship. Samuel's mother took him to the temple when he was a young boy, and he lived there with Eli the high priest. Through the years, as Samuel observed men and women offering their worship to God, he gained a thorough understanding of what it meant that the Israelites were God's people.

One of the defining moments in Samuel's life occurred while he was still a young child: God commissioned him to deliver a rebuke to Eli. Samuel "was afraid to tell Eli the vision" (3:15), but he did divulge all of the details as he had been bidden. Even as a boy, God was preparing this future judge and prophet for the rigors of his leadership role. Samuel loved God and even in childhood began developing the courage and conviction he would need during the difficult days in which he would serve Israel. First Samuel 3:19–4:1 describes Samuel's early influence as Israel's moral leader.

Samuel also served as Israel's judge (7:15–17). He traveled a circuit around Israel settling disputes among the people. The integrity with which he handled this powerful position is demonstrated by the challenge he extended, near the end of his life, to the people whom he had served for so many years (12:1–5). He invited anyone whom he had cheated or wronged to come forward and he promised to rectify the situation. The unanimous response was, "You have not cheated or oppressed us. . . . You have not taken anything from anyone's hand" (verse 4). That's quite a testimony, especially coming from the people themselves.

But Samuel may be best remembered as Israel's king-maker and king-breaker. In obedience to God, Samuel anointed Saul as Israel's first king. But he later told Saul that "your kingdom will not endure . . . because you have not kept the LORD's command" (13:14). Even while Saul was king, Samuel effactually served as Israel's spiritual and moral leader.

— Dr. Sid Buzzell, general editor,
The Leadership Bible, New International Version

LOOKING BEYOND YOUR LIFE

1. Read the evangelist Billy Graham's quote at the beginning of the Setting the Stage section "Two Handed Blessings" on page 65. Why would God's desire for us (and therefore his desire for our dreams) involve influencing other people?

2. Thinking about your answers in "Two-Handed Blessings," who would you like to reach through your dream come true? How do you want to influence them?

3. Break into groups of two or three and discuss this question for each participant: How might her dream reach future generations, even if it doesn't look like there is much influence now? If appropriate, on the board or easel pad create a diagram that shows how this woman's dream can multiply into other people's lives.

4. If a dream is not fulfilled during your lifetime, how can you still reach others for God's kingdom through alternate channels of influence?

5. From what you've learned from and discussed about Hannah, as a group write a list of "Guidelines for Pursuing Dreams." Include three to five points that represent the most important things you want to remember while waiting for and then living a dream come true.

The Bible says, "Those who sow in tears will reap with songs of joy" (Psalm 126:5). So it is worth the effort of "sowing" into our dreams.

To influence others toward God is a great privilege. During our lifetime we may gather up obvious results, we may not. But we can still proclaim, "The LORD has done great things for us, and we are filled with joy" (verse 3). If we entrust our dreams to him, we'll reap eternal benefits.

Prayer Matters

SHARING WHAT WE ENJOY

Ask one group member to read aloud the following adapted prayer of Saint Augustine from the fourth century. How is this an appropriate prayer for people whose dreams have been fulfilled? For those whose dreams haven't been realized?

Close this session by reading Augustine's words again together, as a prayer of dedication. Then the group leader can speak the benediction from Jude 24–25.

Group:

O Lord, our Savior, who has warned us that thou wilt require much of those to whom much is given; grant that we whose lot is cast in so goodly a heritage may strive together the more abundantly by prayer ... and by every other appointed means, to extend to others what we so richly enjoy.

May our lives be to the fulfillment of thy holy will, and our own everlasting salvation; through Jesus Christ our Lord.

Amen.

Leader:

To him who is able to keep you from falling and to present you before his glorious presence without fault and with great joy — to the only God our Savior be glory, majesty, power and authority, through Jesus Christ our Lord, before all ages, now and forevermore! Amen.

After Hours

LOOKING BACK, LOOKING AHEAD

As we pursue our dreams, it helps to look both backward and forward to encourage and inspire us. We look back to see what we've learned and strengthen our faith. We look ahead to reaffirm our calling and stir up hope.

With a friend: Choose a woman who has influenced others for God and create a scrapbook filled with letters of appreciation and mementos from people she's affected. Surprise her with the book on her birthday or another meaningful occasion. (Start a few months ahead of time so people can mail in letters and you can remind the procrastinators.) Be encouraged that your life could be this influential, too!

On your own: On a sheet of paper or index card paste a photo or draw a picture of someone who has influenced your life. In a few sentences explain why this person has impacted you. Title this side of the paper, "Looking Back with Gratitude."

On the opposite side of the sheet, paste or draw a picture of the people you'd like to influence through your dream. Again, write a few sentences that explain why you want to reach them. Title this side of the page, "Looking Ahead with Hope."

Sign the paper and date it, then post it somewhere where you can frequently be reminded of and motivated toward your dream.

Words to Remember

UNTO THE GENERATIONS

One generation will commend your works to another;

they will tell of your mighty acts.

— Psalm 145:4

HANNAH — *Entrusting Your Dreams to God*

Leader's Guide

*T*hese guidelines and suggested answers can help enhance your group's effectiveness. However, remember that many questions require opinions rather than "right" or "wrong" answers. Input is provided only for those questions that may need additional insight.

To guide the group effectively, it helps to complete each session privately before you meet together. Then as you lead the group you can better facilitate the discussion by clarifying the questions when needed, offering suggestions if the conversation lags, drawing out members who aren't contributing much, redirecting the focus from participants who tend to dominate, and asking women for explanation when they contribute simple "yes" or "no" answers. Also, during the prayer time be sensitive to women who need encouragement or ideas for praying as a group.

For all of the sessions use a whiteboard, chalkboard, or easel pad for making lists and comments the entire group can observe. Also provide markers for writing.

SESSION ONE: *The Object of Great Desire*

Objective: To believe in and wait for the
dreams God has planted in our hearts.

Discussing Hannah's Story: Desire Turned into Dilemma

2. (Second question.) We're not told why God closed Hannah's womb, so opinions will vary. Perhaps he wanted to use her barrenness and conception to prove his miraculous power and provision in his people's lives. Or maybe he wanted to work out some things in Hannah's life first. Or perhaps he wanted to be assured that she would offer her son for temple service. That is, God in his omnipotence had already designated Samuel as Israel's moral leader. He needed Samuel's mother

to be willing to dedicate him for a lifetime of service. Mother love runs deep, so prolonged barrenness created a willing heart. On the other hand, who can know the mind of God? His ways are past finding out.

Sharing Your Story: Describing the Desire Within

1. Most of us can identify with Hannah in one way or another. Some possibilities: desiring something we can't seem to obtain; feeling the pain of not fitting in; being misunderstood; not having the support we need; begging God for what we desire; wondering if he will answer our prayers; specifically, longing to have a baby.

3. God speaks to and inspires us toward a dream in ways unique to us. So possible questions we can ask ourselves are: How has God expressed his will to us? Has he confirmed this guidance to us? Do others we trust agree that this is a God-inspired dream? Does this dream line up with how he has spoken to us in the past? Does it line up with Scripture? Does it match our natural talents, spiritual gifts, and inner desires? (God works through the gifting he has given to us.) Are we willing to wait for his timing rather than plunge in too early or compulsively? Can we serve God and others with this dream? Are we expressing the fruit of the Spirit as we pursue it?

Prayer Matters: Gathering Up Hearts and Hope

So you don't break the mood and continuity, before you begin reading the psalm, designate who will say the closing prayer.

SESSION TWO: *A Matter of the Heart*

Objective: To be open to God's changes as we
wait for our dreams to come true.

Discussing Hannah's Story: Transformed in the Temple

2. (Second question.) Some may think Hannah changed significantly, from "bitterness of soul" to surrendering to God. Others may believe she only intensified her request by making a vow to God; she still desperately wanted something from him.

Still others may feel she followed a natural progression in prayer, finally sensing what God desired. Whatever the case, she does seem to change her approach, which may indicate internal changes.

4. (Second question.) The priest was God's representative. Favor with him might mean favor with God.
5. Opinions may vary, but some possibilities are that Hannah had finally fully surrendered to God; she felt reassured by Eli's support and blessing; she may have sensed God's presence and reassurance; or she decided to accept her circumstances.
6. Specific answers will vary, but Hannah's birth of a son seems linked to her surrender in the temple.

Sharing Your Story: First Things First

2. Some suggestions may include asking these questions: Do our motives line up with God's Word? Do we have a clear conscience before God? If we keep our hearts pliable before God (Psalm 51:10), he will reveal our motives. Along with the psalmist, we can ask God to search our hearts and reveal if there is any "offensive way" (Psalm 139:24) or wrong motives in us.
4. Some qualities mentioned may appear in passages such as Romans 12:9–21, 1 Corinthians 13, and Galatians 5:22.

Prayer Matters: A Request for Revelation

Before you begin, designate who will say the closing prayer.

SESSION THREE: *A Promise Kept*

Objective: To grow in and keep
commitments as we pursue our dreams.

Discussing Hannah's Story: The Power of a Pledge

1. One suggestion might be that Hannah wanted to spend as much time as possible with her son before she had to give him up. Another reason may be that visiting the temple would be a painful reminder of the sacrifice to come. Some may wonder, too, if Hannah was struggling with whether she could/ would keep her commitment.

2. Elkanah seems more understanding of his wife, perhaps because he's experienced firsthand how Hannah longed for and now loved this child. He may also have sensed that God's hand was in this mother-son relationship, and he didn't want to interfere beyond his responsibilities. Also, the suggestions for answers in question one could have also applied to Hannah's husband.

3. Elkanah seemed to be a man who respected and kept vows. Verse 21 states that Elkanah made an annual sacrifice "to fulfill his vow." The fact that he didn't override Hannah's vow suggests he loved and respected his wife, and/or he sensed that this promise pleased the Lord. He might also have sensed that their son was destined to be in God's service.

5. (Second question.) Hannah has grown from wanting her own desires to serving God's. Though we don't know how she felt, the text doesn't reveal her as distraught as when she prayed to God for a son.

Sharing Your Story: Factors for Faithfulness

5. If group members are concerned about vows they made and didn't keep, stress that God is full of grace. We may not have realized what we were doing, and he forgives our mistakes. Even if we were serious about a promise, he pardons our sins if we repent. While we don't want to be frivolous about past promises, avoid turning this question into a guilt-provoking time.

Prayer Matters: A Steadfast Heart

Bring enough index cards to the session for each member of your group.

SESSION FOUR: *The Source of Strength*

Objective: To acknowledge God as the
source of our fulfilled dreams.

Discussing Hannah's Story: A Time for Adoration

2. Hannah appears to have grown in her trust and confidence in God. Though it must have been painful giving up her son, she hadn't forgotten that the Lord answered her prayers, and that he is good to his people, especially the forsaken and down-

HANNAH – *Entrusting Your Dreams to God*

trodden. One also wonders if she wasn't touched by God's Spirit at this time, because she praised him with such poetic and jubilant words.

5. The additions to Hannah's prayer made it more prophetic, linking her obedience to important events in Israel's future. She offered up Samuel. Her son then became a gifted moral leader who anointed and advised David, the nation's great king.

Sharing Your Story: Credit When It's Due

2. Suggestions: We can praise God to take our mind off ourselves; to release the work of the Holy Spirit in our lives; to lift our spirits; to be obedient to Scripture; to acknowledge who God is and what he has done; to enjoy the Lord; to wage spiritual warfare; to spiritually strengthen the inner person; to celebrate. Group members may have other suggestions from their experiences with praise. Psalms 146–150 also mention many of the results of praise.

SESSION FIVE: *A Lifetime of Letting Go*

Objective: To be obedient to God while living our dreams.

Discussing Hannah's Story: A Blessing for Obedience

1. Each year Hannah visited the temple with her husband, where she spent time with her son. Each year she had to say goodbye, giving him up again. She also stuck to her commitment to Elkanah and a growing family at home.

2. Hannah could have been worried about Eli's advanced age and ability to train her son; his weak leadership over his sons; their wickedness and disregard for the temple. Would Samuel be affected by all this and fall in with evil people? Would he, too, decide to sleep with women in the temple? Despite all this, Hannah stuck to her commitment, most likely indicating that she trusted God. It could be imagined that when she returned home, she prayed much for her son.

3. Hannah could have felt comforted by the fact that Samuel was in God's service, which was a great honor. And that the presence of Nazirites could bring God's blessing to Israel.

4. Eli seemed grateful that Hannah provided the successor that he needed, a protégé he wouldn't find among his own heirs. He recognized Hannah's sacrifice and wanted God to bless her for it. Also, Israel's future was at stake, and this woman secured its moral leadership.

5. Group members may list many characteristics. Among them can be that God often blesses those who obey him.

Sharing Your Story: The Ongoing Dream

1. Surrendering to God's will as to whether we'll receive our dream is only the first step. God wants us to follow his guidance as we fulfill the dream.

3. When we cultivate a love relationship with the Lord, we obey because we want to please him, rather than out of fear of his punishment (John 14:21). Psalm 112 gives insight to those who fear the Lord and delight in his commands.

SESSION SIX: *A Lingering Influence*

Objective: To use our dreams for God's purposes.

Discussing Hannah's Story: Like Mother, Like Son

1. Samuel was the Lord's next appointed leader for Israel, who already was living in obedience to him. Eli was old and it may have been time to "pass the mantle" on to the next generation. Or perhaps God could no longer trust Eli's judgment and fortitude since his sons lived wickedly. Samuel may have been the only pure heart in the temple. And perhaps God was also honoring Hannah's faith.

2. Eli could have felt jealous and left out. He could have blocked Samuel's access to the Lord, especially since God rarely spoke in those days. But Eli was wise enough (or perhaps resigned enough) to recognize that something important was about to happen through this boy.

4. It seems as though Eli has given up, having tried to rein in his sons but without success. He already knew there would be serious consequences.

Sharing Your Story: Looking Beyond Your Life

1. Though many Bible verses could be suggested, they might include John 3:16, Mark 16:15, and Galatians 5:13.
5. To make the guidelines memorable, you may want each member to write them on special paper, handed out once the list is completed.

WOMEN OF FAITH℠

Women of Faith partners with various Christian organizations,
including Zondervan, Campus Crusade for Christ International,
Crossings Book Club, Integrity Music, International Bible Society,
Partnerships, Inc., and World Vision
to provide spiritual resources for women.

For more information about Women of Faith
or to register for one of our nationwide conferences,
call 1-800-49-FAITH.
www.women-of-faith.com

8/99